Excel Fo... Functions 2020

The Step by Step Excel Guide with Examples on How to Create Powerful Formulas

Adam Ramirez

present accurate, up to date, reliable, complete information. No warranties of any kind are declared or implied. Readers acknowledge that the author is not engaged in the rendering of legal, financial, medical or professional advice. The content within this book has been derived from various sources. Please consult a licensed professional before attempting any techniques outlined in this book.

By reading this document, the reader agrees that under no circumstances is the author responsible for any losses, direct or indirect, that are incurred as a result of the use of the information contained within this document, including, but not limited to, errors, omissions, or inaccuracies.

Table of Contents

vi

Bonus

Grab your free book
https://dl.bookfunnel.com/jen2tkssx7

This book includes an overview on how each formula works along with easy to follow examples. The formulas in this book include Excel 2019 functions and are ideal for beginners through to advanced Excel users.

Get your accounts, calendars, inventory, and budgets working effortlessly with these 50 must know Excel formulas explained in *50 Most Important Formulas in Excel*. Gain valuable knowledge to put into practice and advance your Excel career.

Grab your free book
https://dl.bookfunnel.com/jen2tkssx7

Introduction

Microsoft Excel is a tool that most people use to store, analyze, and retrieve information such as commissions, grades, figures or any other important data connected to their personal or business finances. Excel is an essential tool for documentation and encoding as well.

Most companies use this tool to maintain their business books, budget, fiscal data, and other calculations, but not many people can use MS Excel to its full potential. It can be a bit confusing to use Excel if you are not well versed with the different functions and formulas. Some users only have basic knowledge of Excel but have no clue how to use formulas and functions or minimize the number of formulas they see on the screen.

This book is written with the intent to help you understand Excel like never before. In the course of this book, you will learn the basics of Excel and understand its important functions. By the end of the book, you will learn the most commonly used formulas, functions, charts, and columns which will make your life easy in managing data.

Microsoft Excel is not only used for business; you can use it for your personal finances as well. The book will shed some light on the different forms and types of cell referencing you need to learn. We will look at both relative and absolute cell referencing and learn how to use each of these methods.

It is important to learn these methods so you know how to copy formulas, data, and functions across different cells in a worksheet or workbook.

So, if you are ready to begin, let's dive in and learn. Thank you for purchasing the book. I hope you get the information you are looking for.

Chapter One: An Introduction to Excel

Numerous businesses and individuals across the globe use Microsoft Excel, since it is a great way to get accurate data in a short time. One of the most impressive things about Excel is that you can use it anywhere and for different kinds of work. For example, it can be used for complex tasks such as data management, billing, analysis, finance, inventory, and complex calculations, or you can use it to perform various mathematical functions or your daily budget. It caters to all ends of the user spectrum.

MS Excel offers your file extra security so other users cannot tamper with your data. Excel has become a part of people's lives, and has numerous features and tools. Before we look at the various functions and formulas in Excel, let us look at some of the advantages of using Excel.

Benefits of Using Excel

Storing and Analyzing Data

Most businesses use Excel because they can analyze large volumes of data to identify any trends or correlations. You can store and summarize data using charts and graphs. These graphs and charts will make it easier for you to understand data better. Once you store data in a systematic manner, you can use it for various purposes. This tool makes it easier for you to implement different operations on data using multiple tools.

Easier to Work on Data

Microsoft Excel has many tools that will make your work extremely easy. You can use these tools to search, filter, and sort through data. When you combine these tools with pivot tables or simple tables, you can finish the analysis in very little time. You can look for multiple elements in the data set to answer various questions or problems.

Spreadsheets and Data Recovery

Another use of Excel is that you can recover it without any inconvenience. If you store important information in Excel, and the file gets lost or damaged, you can restore the file using the last copy of that file. Spreadsheets make it easier for people to work with Microsoft Excel. You can reduce the size of a spreadsheet if it occupies too much space on your hard disk.

Mathematical Formulas

Excel helps solve complex mathematical problems without much effort. There are multiple formulas in Excel that allow you to implement operations such as average, VLookup, references, sum, etc. Excel also allows you to perform these functions on multiple variables in the data set. Therefore, most people use Excel if they have to solve complex mathematical problems.

Security

Excel provides an additional layer of security on files and users can protect their data sheets and files using a password.

Sophisticated Visualization

Excel allows you to visualize different data points in the data set in a sophisticated manner. You can highlight the items you want to represent in the visualization to make it easier to present the data. If you store data in Microsoft Excel, and want to highlight only specific parts that are important, you can do this using the features of data presentation in Excel. If you want, you can add more color and features to the spreadsheets where you store data.

Online Access

You can access MS Excel from anywhere using any device. You can work conveniently using this application. Therefore, most businesses prefer working with Excel since they can access the data from any location or device.

Combines Data

You can store your data in one location, which ensures that the data is safe and secure. You can use different spreadsheets to store all the data in one file in MS Excel.

Trend Analysis

Since you can represent various data variables and points in the form of graphs and charts, you can identify different trends within the data set. When you have Microsoft Excel, you can extend trendlines beyond the graph. This helps users analyze various patterns and trends in the data set. Remember, every business wants to identify trends in the data sets so they can determine a method to increase their profits. Through Microsoft Excel, those in business can maximize their profits with ease.

Excel makes it easier for people to manage their expenses. Let us assume that an individual makes around $5,000 every month. He will spend some money on expenses each month, and can analyze this using Excel. This will help him control his expenses accordingly.

Functions and Formulas in Excel

Excel allows you to use multiple formulas (or expressions) to calculate the value of a cell or variable. This application also has many predefined formulas already available in Excel. We will look at some of these in better detail later in the book.

Let us calculate the average of three numbers in cells A1, A2 and A3. To do this, we use a predefined function in Excel called AVERAGE. The function is =AVERAGE(A1:A3).

How to Enter a Formula?

Follow the steps given below to enter a formula in Excel:

Move to the active cell or the cell where you want to enter the formula.

Enter the formula using an equal sign before the variables. For example, if you want to calculate the sum of three variables, you can use the following formula in Excel: =A1+A2+A3.

You can also select the cells A1, A2 and A3, instead of typing them out.

Now, if you change the values in Cells A1, A2, or A3, Excel automatically recalculates the value in Cell A4.

How to Edit a Formula?

If a cell has a formula, Excel shows it in the formula bar when you click on the cell.

Follow the steps given below to edit the formula:

- Select the cell where you want to make a change to the formula.

- Click on the formula bar to make the change.

When you press Enter, Excel automatically calculates the value in the cell

Precedence of Operators

Microsoft Excel uses the BODMAS rule to calculate the formula. If any part of the formula is in parentheses, it calculates the value within the parentheses, and then performs the product, division, multiplication, addition and subtraction functions.

Microsoft Excel uses the BODMAS rule to calculate the formula. If any part of the formula is in parentheses, it calculates the value within the parentheses, and then performs the product, division, multiplication, addition and subtraction functions. Consider the following formula: =A1+A2*A3, where A1, A2 and A3 are cell references.

Excel follows the steps below:

- The first operation performed is the multiplication operation. It first calculates the product (P) of the values in Cells A2 and A3.

It then moves onto the addition operation, where it adds P to the value in Cell A1.

Let us look at another example. Consider the formula: (A1+A2)*A3.

Excel first calculates the sum of the values in Cells A1 and A2 before it multiplies the value to the value in Cell A3.

How to Copy or Paste a Formula?

Excel automatically adjusts the cell references for any new cell when you copy the formula. The references depend on where you copy the formula. Follow the steps given below to understand this better: Let us assume there are numbers in Cells A1, A2, A3, B1, B2, and B3, and there is a formula in Cell A4.

- Copy the formula in Cell A4 into Cell B4.

- Click on CTRL+C on Cell A4 and move to Cell B4. When you right click on the cell,

Excel opens a dialog box that allows you to choose what you want to paste.

- Alternatively, you can click on CTRL+V or drag the formula from Cell A4 to Cell B4. You can also shift the formula using the function CTRL+R.

- Excel automatically changes the cell references and moves the formula to Cell B4.

How to Insert a Function?

Every function has the same syntax. Consider the function used in the first example to calculate the average of three numbers. The function was AVERAGE (A1:A3). Let us break this function down further:

- The word AVERAGE is the name of the function

- The values between the parentheses are the arguments

Based on this function, Excel calculates the average between the numbers in cells A1, A2, and A3. It is difficult to identify which function to use in Excel based on the task, but the Insert function in Excel makes it easier to do this. Perform the steps below to insert a function in Excel:

- Choose the cell where you want to perform the operation.

- Click on the button below to insert a function.

- Excel opens a dialog box, and you can choose the function you want to add depending on the category or task. For this example, let us select the COUNTIF function. This function counts the number of data points depending on some criteria.

- Now click on OK

- Excel now opens the Function Arguments dialog box on the screen. You should select the range, and enter the criteria based on what you need. Click on OK.

- Excel provides the result in the cell where you enter the formula.

Alternatively, you can also type the formula by starting with the equal sign. Once you type the name of the formula, you can enter or select the cells you want to use in the calculation.

The Formula Tab

In this section, we will look at every section in the formula tab.

Function Library

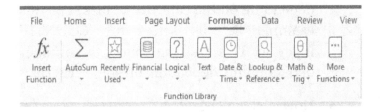

Insert Function: You can use the shortcut Shift+F3 to open the dialog box. If you click on the button, you can open the dialog box to search for a specific function to display the list of functions you can use in Excel.

AutoSum: When you click on this button, Excel inserts a sum function in the cell to automatically calculate the sum of the values in the cells above. The drop down includes commands like Min, Max, Count, and Average. It also includes an option that allows you to select more functions. You can find the same button in the Home Tab.

Recently Used: This dropdown gives you access to the ten functions you recently used in Excel.

Financial: This dropdown gives you access to all financial functions.

Logical: This dropdown gives you access to all logical functions.

Text: This dropdown gives you access to all text functions.

Date and Time: This dropdown gives you access to all the date and time functions.

Lookup and Reference: This dropdown gives you access to all reference and lookup functions.

Math and Trig: This dropdown gives you access to all mathematical and trigonometric functions.

More Functions: This drop down gives you access to various engineering, statistical, compatibility, information, cube and web functions.

We will look at these in further detail later in the book.

Defined Names

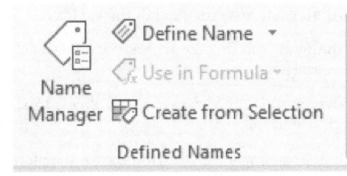

Name Manager: Excel displays a dialog box when you click on this button.

Define Name: This button has a dropdown. When you click on this button, Excel displays a New Name dialog box. The dropdown has the following commands: Define Names and Apply Names. The former allows you to create a name for ranges across workbooks or worksheets. It displays these names in the New Name dialog box. When you click on the Apply Names command, Excel displays a dialog box with different options.

Use in Formula: This button has a drop down that contains the list of every named range in the workbook. It also allows you to paste names. When you click on this option, Excel opens a dialog box.

Create from Selection: Excel displays a dialog box when you click on the button, where you can enter the name for a selected range using the name of the row or column.

Formula Auditing

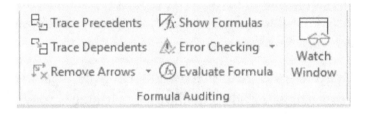

Trace Precedents: Excel draws arrows on the worksheet to show you the cells that affect the value of the active cell.

Trace Dependents: Excel draws arrows that point to the cells in the worksheet or workbook that depend on the value in the active cell.

Remove Arrows: If you click on the buttons mentioned above, Excel draws many arrows on your screen. When you click on this button, Excel removes the arrows on the screen. The dropdown gives you three options: Remove Arrows, Remove Dependent Arrows, and Remove Precedent Arrows.

Show Formulas: This button displays the formula and not the result of that formula.

Error Checking: Excel opens the Error Checking dialog box when you click on this button. If you click on the dropdown, you can choose from the following options: circular references, error checking, and trace error. Excel enables the circular reference option only if there is such an error in your sheet.

Evaluate Formula: Excel displays the Evaluate Formula dialog box that allows you to step through every calculation in the function.

Watch Window: This button displays the watch window where you can view the content of every cell and see how the values change.

Calculation

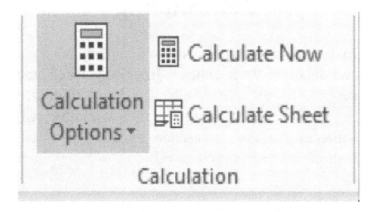

Calculation Options: When you click on this dropdown, Excel allows you to change the calculation setting in the workbook between Automatic, Automatic except for Data Tables and Manual. This is an application setting.

Calculate Now: Use the button 'F9' to calculate the formula in a cell. This does not appear in a dialog box.

Calculate Sheet: This button allows you to calculate all the formulas in the sheet.

Chapter Two: The Basics of Relative and Absolute Cell Referencing

Excel allows two types of cell referencing: absolute and relative. Both behave differently when you copy them into other cells. A relative reference changes when you copy the formula to another cell, while an absolute reference remains the same regardless of where you copy it.

Relative References

Every cell reference in Excel is relative by default. When we copied the formula from Cell A4 to Cell B4 in the previous chapter, the formula changed automatically based on the relative position of the values. It is easier to use relative referencing when you perform the same calculations across various columns and rows.

How to Create and Copy the Formula Using a

Relative Reference

In the example below, let us look at how to create a formula in one row and use the same formula across other rows in the file. Instead of creating a new formula for every row, we can create a single formula in cell C4 and copy it in the other rows. Let us look at the steps to follow to do this:

Consider the screenshot below. You can see a formula in cell C4.

F2			f_x	=(B2+C2+D2+E2)/4		
	A	B	C	D	E	F	G
1		Mathematics	Social Studies	English	Science	Average	
2	Student A	79	60	77	79	73.75	
3	Student B	58	61	72	66		
4	Student C	65	56	76	50		
5	Student D	66	71	55	68		
6	Student E	70	59	57	52		
7	Student F	58	58	67	59		
8							
9							

In the image above, the formula in cell F2 calculates the average of the marks that a student scored in four subjects. When you enter the formula, Excel displays the result in cell F2.

Now move to cell F2 and find the fill handle. This is located at the bottom-right corner of the active cell.

F2					fx	=(B2+C2+D2+E2)/4	
	A	B	C	D	E	F	G
1		Mathematics	Social Studies	English	Science	Average	
2	Student A	79	60	77	79	73.75	
3	Student B	58	61	72	66		
4	Student C	65	56	76	50		
5	Student D	66	71	55	68		
6	Student E	70	59	57	52		
7	Student F	58	58	67	59		
8							
9							

Now click on the handle, and drag the formula across the remaining cells, until cell F7. When you release the mouse, you see that Excel copies the formula to selected cells using the relative reference. This displays the result in the remaining cells.

A	B	C	D	E	F	G
	Mathematics	Social Studies	English	Science	Average	
Student A	79	60	77	79	73.75	
Student B	58	61	72	66		
Student C	65	56	76	50		
Student D	66	71	55	68		
Student E	70	59	57	52		
Student F	58	58	67	59		

| F3 | | ▼ | : | × | ✓ | f_x | =(B3+C3+D3+E3)/4 |

▲	A	B	C	D	E	F
1		Mathematics	Social Studies	English	Science	Average
2	Student A	79	60	77	79	73.75
3	Student B	58	61	72	66	64.25
4	Student C	65	56	76	50	61.75
5	Student D	66	71	55	68	65
6	Student E	70	59	57	52	59.5
7	Student F	58	58	67	59	60.5

You can see that Excel copied the formula into the cells below.

You can also double click on each of the cells to check the accuracy of the formulas. The relative reference for each cell should be different depending on the rows.

Absolute References

You may not always want the cell reference to change if you copy the formula to other cells. As mentioned earlier, absolute reference does not change when you copy the formula from one cell to another. Most people use absolute reference if they want to keep a column or row constant.

If you want to use absolute reference, you should add the dollar sign before the column and row. You can use the symbol either for the entire reference or before the row and column.

$A$2	The row and column do not change
$A2	The column does not change
A$2	The row does not change

People often use the $A$2 format if they create formula using absolute cell referencing, but they do not use the other two formats often. Press the F4 key to create an absolute reference when you write the formula. You can use this key to switch between relative referencing and the different formats of absolute referencing.

How to Create and Copy Formula Using Absolute Referencing?

In the following example, we use the value in cell H2 to calculate the percentage of the marks scored by each student. Since the value in cell H2 must remain constant, and we only want to use the value in that cell, we use absolute referencing. When you do this, you see that the formula does not change.

First, choose the cell where you want to include the formula. Now, enter the formula. In our example, we first calculate the sum of the scores and then the percentage. The formula is =F2/$H$1, and we make $H$1 an absolute reference since the value must remain constant.

COUNTIF	▼	×	✓	f_x	=F2/$H$1			
◢	A	B	C	D	E	F	G	H	I
1		Mathematics	Social Studies	English	Science	Sum	Percentag	400	
2	Student A	79	60	77	79	295	=F2/$H$1		
3	Student B	58	61	72	66	257			
4	Student C	65	56	76	50	247			
5	Student D	66	71	55	68	260			
6	Student E	70	59	57	52	238			
7	Student F	58	58	67	59	242			
8									

Excel calculates the result and displays it in the cell.

Now move to cell G2 and find the fill handle. This is located at the bottom-right corner of the active cell. Now, drag the formula across the column until G7. When you release the cursor, you can see the formula in the cells. Note that the reference of cell H1 is an absolute reference.

G2		✕	✓	f_x	=F2/$H$1			
	A	B	C	D	E	F	G	H
1		Mathematics	Social Studies	English	Science	Sum	Percentag	400
2	Student A	79	60	77	79	295	74%	
3	Student B	58	61	72	66	257		
4	Student C	65	56	76	50	247		
5	Student D	66	71	55	68	260		
6	Student E	70	59	57	52	238		
7	Student F	58	58	67	59	242		
8								

G4		✕	✓	f_x	=F4/$H$1			
	A	B	C	D	E	F	G	H
1		Mathematics	Social Studies	English	Science	Sum	Percentag	400
2	Student A	79	60	77	79	295	74%	
3	Student B	58	61	72	66	257	64%	
4	Student C	65	56	76	50	247	62%	
5	Student D	66	71	55	68	260	65%	
6	Student E	70	59	57	52	238	60%	
7	Student F	58	58	67	59	242	61%	
8								
9								
10								

If you want to check the accuracy of the formula, double click on the cell. Check whether the reference of cell H1 is absolute in each row.

Remember to include the dollar sign when you make an absolute reference in cells in Excel. In the example below, we do not use the dollar sign, and this makes Excel use a relative reference. This produces an incorrect result in the cells below.

G3			f_x	=F3/H2			
	A	B	C	D	E	F	G	H
1		Mathematics	Social Studies	English	Science	Sum	Percentag	400
2	Student A	79	60	77	79	295	74%	
3	Student B	58	61	72	66	57	#DIV/0!	
4	Student C	65	56	76	50	247	#DIV/0!	
5	Student D	66	71	55	68	260	#DIV/0!	
6	Student E	70	59	57	52	238	#DIV/0!	
7	Student F	58	58	67	59	242	#DIV/0!	

Mixed Cell Referencing

Mixed cell referencing, as the name suggests, is a mix of both absolute and relative cell referencing. We looked at the two variations in the above section.

Chapter Three:
Understanding Functions

Financial

This is where we begin our journey through the different formulas. The financial formulas are extremely important since they encompass different functions that you can use to understand business and personal finances better. The financial function library has multiple functions you can use to perform a variety of financial functions. Let us consider some of the most important ones:

Future Value

You can calculate the future value of any investment that has a periodic payment and constant interest rate using the future value formula. The formula uses the following syntax:

FV(Rate, Nper, [Pmt], PV, [Type]), where

- The rate is the interest period or rate

- Nper is the number of periods

- [Pmt] is the period or payment

- PV is the present value of the amount

- [Type] indicates when you make the payment - either at the start or end of the period

Example

Let us assume that A invested $1000 in 2016 and makes a yearly payment. What would the future value of this principle be in 2019 if the interest is 10%? The equation in Excel is:

=FV(10%, 3, 1, -1000)

= $1700

FVSCHEDULE

You can use this function to calculate the value of a loan or bond with a variable interest. The syntax of this function is:

FVSCHEDULE (Principal, Schedule), where

- Principal is the current value of the investment

- Schedule is the interest rate that you add to Excel. You must include this as a range, which means you consider all interest rates together. When you use this function in Excel, use different cells and select the range in this section

Example

Let us assume that P invests $100, written in cell C1, at the end of the year 2016, and the interest rate changes every year. The rates are 4$, 6% and 5% and written in cells C2, C3 and C4 for the years 2017, 2018, and 2019 written in cells B2, B3 and B4, respectively. The future value in 2019 is:

=FVSCHEDULE(C1, C2:c4)

=$115.72

Present Value

Now that you know how to calculate the future value, let us look at the formula to calculate the present value. The syntax of this formula is

PV(Rate, Nper, [Pmt], FV, [Type]), where

- The rate is the interest period or rate

- Nper is the number of periods

- [Pmt] is the period or payment

- FV is the future value of the amount

- [Type] indicates when you make a payment - either at the start or end of the period

Example

Let us assume that the future value of an investment in 2019 is $100, and the individual makes a yearly payment with an interest rate of 10%. What would the present value be now?

=PV(10%, 3, 1, -100)

=$72.64

Net Present Value

The net present value of any investment is the sum of all the cash flows, both positive and negative, over the years. The function uses the following syntax in Excel,

=NPV(Rate, Value 1, [Value 2], [Value 3], ...), where

- The rate parameter represents the discount rate for a period

- The values represent the positive and negative cash flows, where you consider the negative values as positive inflows and positive values as outflows

Example

Calculate the NPV using the following data:

Details	In US $
Rate of Discount	5%
Initial Investment	-1000
Return from 1st year	300
Return from 2nd year	400
Return from 3rd year	400
Return from 4th year	300

To calculate the NPV in Excel, enter the following formula:

	A	B	C	D	E
1					
2		Details	In US $		
3		Rate of Discount	5%		
4		Initial Investment	-1000		
5		Return from 1st year	300		
6		Return from 2nd year	400		
7		Return from 3rd year	400		
8		Return from 4th year	300		
9					
10		=NPV(C3,C5:C8)+C4			
11					
12					

=NPV(5%, B4:B7) + B3

= $240.87

XNPV

This function is similar to the NPV function, but the difference between the two is that the income, payment, and cashflow amounts are not periodic. When you write the formula in Excel, you can enter the dates when you make the payment. The syntax of the function is as follows:

XNPV(Rate, Values, Dates), where

- The rate defines the discount rate of the payment for a period

- Values represent the cash flow amounts

- Dates include an array of dates. You can enter the range where you have the cells written in Excel

Example

Calculate the NPV of the following values using the XNPV function:

Details	In US $	Dates
Rate of Discount	5%	
Initial Investment	-1000	1st December 2011
Return from 1st year	300	1st January 2012
Return from 2nd year	400	1st February 2013
Return from 3rd year	400	1st March 2014

Return from 4th year	300	1st April 2015

Write the following function in Excel:

	A	B	C	D	E
1					
2		Details	In US $		
3		Rate of Discount	5%		
4		Initial Investment	-1000	1-Dec-11	
5		Return from 1st year	300	1-Jan-12	
6		Return from 2nd year	400	1-Feb-13	
7		Return from 3rd year	400	1-Mar-14	
8		Return from 4th year	300	1-Apr-15	
9					
10		=XNPV(C3,C4:C8,D4:D8)			
11					
12					

=XNPV(5%, B2:B6, C2:C6)

=$289.90

PMT

The function PMT calculates the periodic payment you must make when you pay off a certain amount of money with a constant interest rate for the period. The syntax of this function is:

=PMT(Rate, Nper, PV, [FV], [Type])

- The rate is the interest period or rate that you pay

- Nper is the number of periods under consideration

- PV is the present value

- [FV] represents the future value of the loan. This an optional value, and you do not have to enter it

- [Type] is another optional value that determines when you make the payments – either at the start or end of the period

Example

Let us assume that you took a loan for $1000 for three years, with an interest rate of 10%. You must make yearly payments. You can calculate the PMT using the following function:

=PMT(10%, 3, 1000)

=402.11

There are many other functions that help you assess the financial situation of the market when you are trying to invest or buy. You could use the different functions like ACCRINT and DB. Use these functions to determine the interest you accrue when you invest in a share.

Logical

These functions are very important when you are trying to choose between two or more investments.

Let us say that you have to choose between a portfolio of shares or buying a house. Before you make the purchase, you must calculate how much you should invest and calculate the profit you make from the investment. Chances are that you do not gain anything. You can use different logical functions to make these comparisons. The following are the types of logical functions in Excel.

AND: This function checks if every argument within the parentheses is true or not. When the function certifies that all the arguments are true, it submits the result true. When you use this function, Excel determines if every variable or value in the parentheses is true.

FALSE: Excel only returns the value FALSE when you use this function.

IF: This function allows you to check the condition by comparing two values or variables. Excel performs different functions depending on whether the condition is true or false.

IFERROR: Excel returns a specific value if the expression is wrong. Excel runs through the next statements if the expression is incorrect.

NOT: This logical formula helps you change the value of the variable to the opposite. This means that everything true changes to false and vice versa.

OR: This function checks if the values are either true or false.

TRUE: This function returns the true value regardless of the variable or function used.

Using the AND function in Excel

As mentioned earlier, the AND function is the most popular function in the logical functions list. The

AND function helps you determine if the value in a cell meets all criteria. It tests the condition you enter and returns the value if the condition is true. The syntax of the function is as follows:

=AND(Logical1, [Logical2], ...)

You must enter the first logical condition, but the other conditions are only optional. Let us now look at some examples of how to use the AND function in Excel.

Formula	Description
=AND(A2="Apples", B2>C2)	This function returns the value TRUE if the cell A2 contains the value Apples and the value of B2 is greater than C2. It returns false otherwise.
=AND(C2>20, C2=B2)	This function returns TRUE if the value of cell C2 is greater than 20, and if the values of cells B2 and C2 are equal. It returns false otherwise.
=AND(A2="Apples", C2>=30, C2>B2)	This function returns the value TRUE if the cell A2 contains the value Apples, the value of C2 is greater than or equal to 30 and its value

	is greater than B2. It returns false otherwise.

Common Uses

The AND function does not have too much use unless you use it with other functions. AND can extend the capability and functionality of a worksheet significantly when used with other functions. A common use of this function is its use in the IF condition to test various functions instead of one. For instance, you can nest more than one AND function within this function.

BETWEEN Condition

Most people use the AND function to check different conditions in the IF logical test. Let us understand this better using the following example. You have three values in the Columns A, B and C. The objective is to determine if the values in these columns are similar. All you have to do is combine the IF and AND function to perform the operation.

OR Function

You can use the OR function to compare two statements or values. The difference between these functions is that this function returns the value 'TRUE' even if one of the conditions is true. The OR function uses the same syntax as the AND function:

= OR(logical1, [logical2], ...)

Like the AND statement, you should enter the first logical statement. Let us look at some examples:

Formula	Description
=OR(A2="Bananas", A2="Oranges")	This function returns TRUE if the value in cell A2 is either oranges or bananas.
=OR(B2>=40, C2>=20)	This function returns TRUE if the value in cell B2 is greater than or equal to 40 or the value in cell C2 is equal to 20.
=OR(B2=" ", C2="")	This function returns the value TRUE if the value in either B2 or C2 is blank or both.

You can use the OR function with other functions to improve the usefulness of the function.

XOR Function

The developers of Excel introduced this function in the 2013 version of Excel. This is also known as the Logical Executive OR function. If you know computer science or a programming language, you'll be familiar with this function. Executive OR is a difficult function to understand if you have never used it before, but let us look at the example below to give it a try. This function also follows a syntax similar to the OR function. The syntax is:

= XOR(logical1, [logical2], ...)

As mentioned earlier, the first logical statement is necessary while the others are optional. The XOR statement contains two statements and returns either TRUE or FALSE. The former value returns TRUE if the arguments or conditions are true, while it returns the latter if the value is false.

Let us look at some examples to understand this better:

Formula	Result	Description
=XOR(1>0, 2<1)	TRUE	This function returns TRUE since the first argument holds true while the second is FALSE.
=XOR(1<0, 2<1)	FALSE	This function returns FALSE since both arguments are FALSE.
=XOR(1>0, 2>1)	FALSE	This function returns FALSE since the arguments are both TRUE.

If you add more logical functions to this function, then you notice the following:

- The function returns TRUE if the number of arguments is odd, and odd arguments are TRUE.

- The function returns FALSE if the number of statements that hold TRUE are even.

If you do not know how the function works, consider the following example: Let us assume you have many contestants and also the results of the first few games. Calculate the scores of each player to determine who enters the next round. Use the following criteria to determine who goes to the next round:

- The contestants who lost the first two rounds cannot enter the third round

- Any contestant who won either the first or second game plays again to determine who moves to the third round

You can use a simple XOR formula to perform this calculation.

NOT Function

As mentioned earlier, this is one of the simplest functions in Excel. The syntax of this function is: =NOT(logical). Excel reverses the value of the argument in the parentheses. In simple words, this function returns TRUE if the NOT function returns

FALSE and vice versa. Consider the following examples:

=NOT(TRUE)

=NOT(2*6=14)

In the first case, Excel returns FALSE and in the second case it returns TRUE. Why do you think anybody would want such a result? In some situations, you may want to know if a specific value does not meet a certain condition. For instance, when you review a list of clothes, you may want to get rid of those colors that do not suit you. To do this, use the NOT formula. If you want to get rid of every piece of clothing that is black, write the following formula in Excel:

=NOT(C2="Black")

| E2 | | f_x | =NOT(C2="black") | |

	A	B	C	D	E
1	Item	Description	Color	Price	Any color but black
2	113456	Coat	White	$980	TRUE
3	113457	Coat	Black	$1,090	FALSE
4	113458	Jacket	Brown	$780	TRUE
5	113459	Fur coat	White	$1,000	TRUE
6	113460	Fur coat	Ivory	$1,035	TRUE
7	113461	Jacket	Black	$760	FALSE
8	113462	Coat	White	$800	TRUE

49

You can perform this function using the Not Equal to operator as well. If you were to use this operator, the formula is: =C2<>"Black". Excel allows you to use the NOT function in conjunction with the other logical functions, such as AND and OR. Let us assume that you want to exclude those clothes that are both black and white. The formula changes to:

=NOT(OR(C2="Black", C2="White"))

If you want to consider a coat in black, but no other clothing, you can use a combination of AND and NOT. The formula changes to:

=NOT(AND(C2="Black", B2="Coat")

Another use of this function is to change the behavior of other functions in Excel. For example, you can combine the ISBLANK and NOT functions to create a new formula in Excel. The function ISBLANK returns TRUE when there is no data in a specific cell. It returns FALSE if you add the NOT function before the ISBLANK function. You can nest a conditional statement like 'IF' in the NOT and ISBLANK function to perform a complex task. Consider the example below:

=IF(NOT(ISBLANK(C2)), C2*0.15, "No bonus :(")

	A	B	C	D	E
				=IF(NOT(ISBLANK(C2)), C2*0.15, "No bonus :(")	

	A	B	C	D	E
1	Salesman	Primary sales	Extra sales	Bonus	
2	Andrew	$1,860	$169	$25	
3	Billy	$910	$145	$22	
4	Erik	$1,020		No bonus :(	
5	Josh	$1,070	$185	$28	
6	Mike	$1,100		No bonus :(	
7	Steve	$1,020	$180	$27	

The above formula does the following:

- Excel first checks if there is a value in cell C2

- If there is a number, it multiplies it by 0.15

When it does this, Excel adds a bonus to those salesmen who have extra sales. If there is no value in C2, Excel adds the text 'No bonus :(' to the cell.

These are some of the ways in which you can use logical functions. Remember, these are basic examples and do not cover the capabilities of various logical functions. It is only when you understand these basics that you can extend your knowledge to tackle complex tasks. You can write elaborate functions to perform these tasks.

Text

You can use the different formulas in this library on the text found in the worksheet or workbook.

Left

This function extracts the characters at the left end of the sentence. The syntax of this function is: =left(text, num_char) where the text is the sentence or the cell containing the sentence and num_char is the number of characters you want to extract from the leftmost end of the sentence. You can use the Right function in the same manner to extract the rightmost end of the sentence.

Len

This function returns the length of the string in a cell. This means it returns the number of characters in the sentence, including the spaces. The syntax of this function is =len(text).

Mid

You can use this function to extract a set of characters from between the sentences. The syntax of this function is: =MID(text, start_char, num_chars) where start_char points to the variable or character from where Excel should begin the extraction and the num_chars parameter determines the number of parameters to extract.

Find

This function finds the position of a specific character in the sentence or string. The syntax of this function is: =FIND(find_text, within_text, [start_num]) where find_text is the character or word you are looking for, within_text is the sentence where you want to look for the character and [start_num] is an optional parameter.

Proper

This function in Excel capitalizes every word in the string or converts the text into the proper case. The syntax of this function is =PROPER(Text).

Rept

This function calculates the number of times a specific text or character appears in a sentence. The syntax of the function is =REPT(Text, number_times).

Trim

This function removes unnecessary spaces at the start and end of the string. The syntax is =TRIM(text).

Upper

This function converts the entire text into upper case from its lower case. The syntax of the function is =UPPER(Text).

Substitute

This function substitutes an existing piece of text or string with a new string or text. The syntax of this function is =SUBSTITUTE (text, old_text, new_text, instance number).

Concatenate

This function joins text together. The syntax is =CONCATENATE(text1, text2,....)

Date and Time

This library has all the functions that perform operations on date and time. The functions in this library provide a lot of information about the dates and times in the sheet. Let us look at some of these functions to understand them better.

Year, Month and Day

These functions give you the year, month, or day using the date entered in the cell. If you have the date 6/23/2020 in cell A1 and you want to extract the year, enter the following formula: =YEAR(A1). Use the formulas MONTH and DAY if you want to extract only the month and day from the date.

Adding Days

You can use the simple addition method to add a few days to the date. Let us assume you have the date 6/23/2020 in cell A1, and you want to add 5 days to the date. Use the following formula to do this: =A1+5.

Date Function

Use the DATE function if you want to add the number of months, days, or years to the function.

This function accepts three arguments – day, month, and year. Since Excel knows how many days there are in a month, it rolls the extra days over to the next month.

Current Time and Date

Excel returns the current time and date using the NOW function. You can use the TODAY function to instruct Excel to return the current date.

Minute, Second, and Hour

You can use the HOUR, MINUTE, or SECOND functions to obtain the hour, minute or seconds in the time, respectively.

Time

Use the time function to add the number of hours, minutes, or seconds to the time.

Lookup and Reference

There are two main formulas called VLOOKUP and HLOOKUP in this list. They are the perfect tools that you can use when you are trying to identify a particular part of the data. Use VLOOKUP when you work with vertical sections of the data set, and HLOOKUP when you work with horizontal sections of the data set.

VLOOKUP

The Vertical Lookup or VLOOKUP function looks for a specific value in the leftmost column of the table. It then returns the value from another column in the same row. Let us look at how to use this function.

Let us assume we have a list of product IDs in Column A and we want to map these IDs to a product in Column G. To do this, we use the VLOOKUP function to look for the ID in the leftmost column in the range E – G (that consists of Product ID, brand, and product, respectively) and return the rightmost value in the range $E$4:$G$7. We set the last parameter to FALSE in case the function returns an error. You can drag the formula in column B, all the way down to the last cell.

Remember, the absolute reference stays the same in the formula above. This means you need to change the reference to a relative reference, so you can drag the function down.

HLOOKUP

This function is similar to the VLOOKUP function, but it performs a horizontal lookup.

Match

This function returns the position of the value or text in a specific range. You obtain the index of the function. Consider the following table.

Green
Blue
Yellow
White

If you had the same content in Excel, and wanted to find the position of Yellow in the list, enter the formula =MATCH("Yellow", Range, 0). The third parameter in the function is optional, and you can either set this value to FALSE or 0, so you do not receive an error.

Excel enters the result 3 in the cell with the formula

Index

This function checks for the position of a variable in a two-dimensional range.

You can also use this function to return the specific value in a one-dimensional range.

You can improve the functionality or use of the INDEX function using the MATCH function.

Choose

This function returns one value from a list or range of values based on the index number.

Mathematical and Trigonometric

This library includes both simple and complex mathematical functions used in Excel. You can perform numerous mathematical and trigonometric processes using this function. Let us look at some of the common mathematical functions.

SUM

You can use this function to add the values in a group of cells or range. The syntax of this formula is: =SUM(cell address : cell address). For example, =SUM(A1:B3) calculates the sum of the values of the cells within the range A1 and B3. Let us assume you want to calculate the total number of hours employees work each day.

Follow the steps given below to do this:

- Choose the cell where you want to add the formula and type the equal sign.

- Now, write the name of the function. Now, select or write the range of the cells you want to use to calculate the sum. Alternatively, drag the mouse across the range.

- Excel calculates the result when you click enter.

You can also use the function in other ways. Most people enter the cell addresses manually to calculate the sum. Alternatively, you can write the numbers within the parentheses to calculate the sum. For example, you can write =SUM(1, 2, 3) = 6.

SUMIF

Continuing with the example above, let us calculate the number of hours female employees spend in the office. The SUMIF function is an easy way to calculate this.

The syntax of this function is =SUMIF(criteria range, criteria, sum range). Let us assume that the criteria (Gender) is in Column B and the number of hours is in Column F. The function will be: =SUMIF(B2:B100, "Female", D2:D100).

You can see the result in the cell where you enter the formula.

AVERAGE

Let us assume we want to calculate the average of the number of hours every employee works in the office. You can use the function AVERAGE to do this. The syntax is =AVERAGE(range). You can see the result when you press the enter key.

You can use the AVERAGEIF() and AVERAGEIFS() functions in the same way as the SUMIF() and SUMIFS() functions.

COUNT

The count function calculates the number of employees or non-blank records in a column or list. The syntax is =COUNT(Range).

ROUND

You can use this function to round off the value in a cell to the nearest number of digits. The syntax of this function is: =ROUND(number, number_of_digits).

RAND

Excel returns a random number between 0 and 1 when you use this function. The syntax of this function is =RAND().

MOD

You can use this function to calculate the remainder of the values in cells when you divide one number with the other. The syntax of this function is =MOD(number, divisor).

INT

You can use this function to convert a decimal number into its integer value. This integer value is less than the decimal number. The syntax of this function is =INT(decimal number).

ABS

This function returns the modulus or absolute value of any number. Regardless of whether the number is positive or negative, it returns the positive value of the number.

ARABIC()

You can use this function to convert any Roman numeral in Excel to Arabic. The function accepts Roman numerals as the argument.

CEILING.MATH()

You can use this function to round any number to the nearest integer. You can also round it off to the nearest significant multiple. This function takes three arguments – number, significance and mode. The number is the number whose ceiling you want to find, the significance is the multiple and mode is also a number. Let us assume we want to calculate the ceiling of the number 6.423. To do this, we write the function =CEILING.MATH(6.423, 2, 5).

More Functions

The last part of the function library contains a lot of other functions you can use in Excel. This list includes different statistical and engineering functions to perform a variety of functions. The first option under this list is statistical functions, and these functions include numerous distribution and central tendency functions. Some of these include:

1. Mean

2. Median

3. Mode

4. Distribution

5. Standard Normal

6. Chi Square and more

You can also use the standard deviation and variance functions to check the difference between the data points in the data set. These functions help you analyze trends and correlations. Some of these statistical functions also help you understand the different forms and types of data. There are certain distributions that you could use to compare two different types of investment.

Statistical Functions

Median

The Median function in Excel calculates the middle number or median in a data set. You must organize the data set either in ascending or descending order, otherwise Excel gives you an incorrect result.

Mode

The mode is the number that occurs frequently in a data set. Use the MODE function in Excel to find this number.

Standard Deviation

The standard deviation is a statistical measure to calculate the deviation of variables in the data set from the mean or average. This measure helps to determine the skewness of the distribution.

Min

This function identifies the minimum value in a set of numbers.

Max

This function identifies the maximum value in a set of numbers.

Large

This function is similar to the MAX function, but the difference is that you can enter a parameter to see the second largest number, third largest number and so on.

Small

This function is similar to the MIN function, but the difference is that you can enter a parameter to see the second smallest number, third smallest number and so on.

The next is the Engineering functions which has a list of different equations every engineer uses or studies. You can use these equations to answer any technical questions about the data set. Most users do not use these functions.

When you try to extend your knowledge and work on complex functions, you may make mistakes. If you cannot identify the mistake when you glance at the formula, use the Formula Auditing tab. Either evaluate the formula or check for any errors. The latter does not always work since it does not consider a null or incorrect value as an error in the formula. Therefore, it is best to use the Evaluate Formula option. You can step into every iteration and see how Excel interprets your formula.

Chapter Four: Tips to Bear in Mind

Excel confuses people quite often, and the functions and formulas tend to confuse them even more. In the previous chapter, we looked at different Excel functions and how you can use those functions to perform different operations. You can use these functions to analyze data and determine the value of the data in the cells. Therefore, it is important you understand how to use these formulas better.

Here are some easy formula and formatting tricks that you can keep in mind.

Computing GDPs

You can use Excel to show the GDP or Gross Domestic Product of countries. Unfortunately, the data is unreadable in its raw form. To understand the data better, you should use different functions and formulas. For example:

China - 7.20378E + 12

France - 2.77552E + 12

Japan - 5,870360E + 12

United States - 1.49913E + 13

You cannot understand these variables easily, but you can use the following functions to understand these numbers better. Convert these numbers into decimals, percentages, or currencies.

Currency

If you want to convert the above data into currency, click Ctrl + Shift + $. The result of the function is:

China - $7,203, 780.00

France - $2, 775, 520.00

Japan - $5, 870, 360.00

United States - $1, 499, 130.00

Decimal Places

If you want to convert the value in decimal places, click Ctrl + Shift + !. This shortcut gives you the following results:

China - 7,203, 780.00

France - 2, 775, 520.00

Japan - 5, 870, 360.00

United States - 1, 499, 130.00

Percentage

To change the data to percentages, click Ctrl + Shift
+ %. This gives you the percentage ranking of the
countries in the list.

China - 10%

France - 4%

Japan - 8%

United States - 21%

Editing Text with Formulas

The previous chapter includes some text functions
you can use on various sentences in Excel.
Consider the example below where the original text

is 'the quick brown fox,' 'JUMPED OVER' and 'LAZY DOG.' These phrases are in the cells A1, B1, and C1, respectively.

So, what function would you use if you want to pull out the first ten characters from the text? You can use the Left function in the following manner: =(LEFT(A1,10).

When you enter this function in Excel, you see the phrase 'the quick' in A2 when you enter the formula. Now, to get the last three rightmost letters from C1, you should type: =(RIGHT (C1,3).

When you do this, you see that the last three letters in cell C1 are now in cell A3.

Number of Characters

You can calculate the number of characters in a certain cell using the LEN formula. We looked at this formula in the previous chapter.

For example, you want to know the number of characters in C1. You simply have to input **=LEN(C1)** in your desired cell, and you see a number of characters in C1.

Sum

The Sum formula is one of the easiest to use. You simply have to input the number of cells that you want to add.

For example, you are using cells A1 to A15.

=SUM(A1, A7) would give you the value of cells A1 and A7

=SUM(A1:A7) would give you the value of cells A1 TO A7

=SUM (A1:A15) would give you the sum total of cells A1 to A15

We have looked at this formula in the previous chapter. You can use other variations of this formula if you want to include some criteria to calculate the sum. Excel has a sumproduct function you can use to calculate the product and sum of values in two columns.

Counting Numbers

You can calculate the number of cells with numbers in a range. To do this, use the formula =COUNT(Range). Excel will only give you the number of cells that have data in them. If any cell does not have information, Excel does not consider it.

You can use the COUNTA function to calculate the number of non-blank cells in the spreadsheet or range. This function also works on text values. Write the following formula to count the number of non-blank cells in the range A1 to A15: =COUNTA(A1:A15).

When you press enter, Excel shows you the exact number of cells in the range with data. Again, this function does not consider blank cells.

IF Statements

Many people use the IF function or statement in Microsoft Excel, and they use these functions to check the criteria. As mentioned earlier, IF is a logical Excel function, and it helps to determine if the data in the sheet meets a certain requirement or criteria. Look at the examples below:

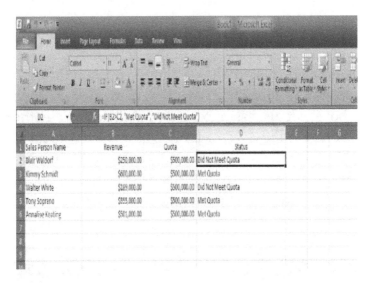

As the example shows, the target quota of every salesperson on the list is $500,000.00. You need to input the following formula to meet the quota: =IF(B2>C2, "Met Quota", "Didn't Meet Quota"). Excel executes the formula and displays the results in Column D. You can see from the results that two of those people did not meet their quota. This formula is extremely helpful when you try to liquidate assets and view the financial status.

SUMIF, COUNTIF, AVERAGEIF

We covered these formulas in the previous chapter. You can use these formulas to determine the estimated value of the data in the range if the data meets the criteria. Continuing with the example above, let us assume you want to calculate the average value only for those salespeople who meet the criteria. You only have to enter the following formula =AVERAGEIF(D2:D6 "Met Quota", B2:B6), and Excel prints the average value in cell B7.

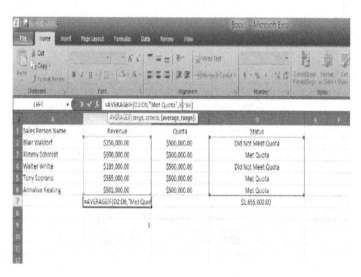

If you want to calculate the sum, you can do this in a similar manner. You must enter the following function: =SUMIF(D2:D6, "Met Quota",B2:B6), and Excel displays the sum in cell D7.

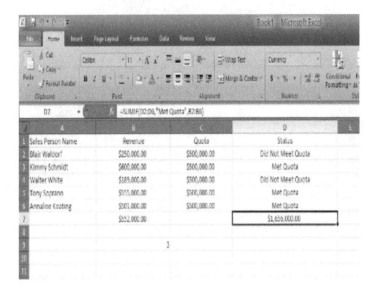

If you want to see how many cells or data points met the criteria, that is, you want to look at the number, use the COUNTIF function. Enter the following formula =COUNTIF(D2:D6, "Met Quota) to display the number of salespeople who met the criteria.

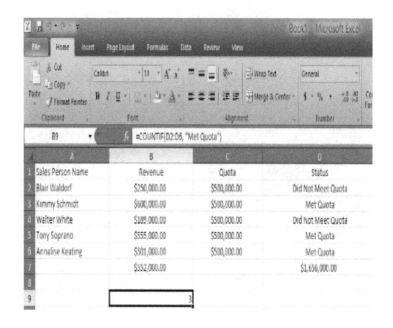

Concatenate

You can also merge information from two different cells into one by using **Concatenate**.

Let us assume that the names HARRY and POTTER are in two cells, A1 and B1, respectively. Now, to put them in just one cell, you have to type **=CONCATENATE (A1," ",B1)**, and the merged name appears in the cell where you enter the formula.

Looking for Information

As mentioned earlier, you can use the **VLOOKUP** formula to detect information from a long list of data. This works best to look for dates of birth, dates when a person entered the school or the office, and other important information.

Take, for example, the kids from Hogwarts. Look at the example below.

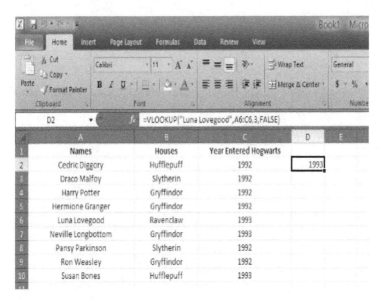

You want to look for the year when Luna Lovegood entered Hogwarts. You simply have to input **=VLOOKUP("LunaLovegood,A6:C6,3,FAL SE)**, and Excel automatically pulls up the year she joined school. In this case, 1993. Again, this works best for long and continuous data.

Chapter Five: Some Excel Shortcuts

You can make the most of Excel if you use the right shortcuts.

Time and Date

To put the current time into a cell, all you have to do is click **Ctrl + Shift + :**

Meanwhile, to put the current date in a cell, go and click **Ctrl + ;** and you are all set.

AutoFill

Autofill is one of the most neglected shortcuts out there. People often forget they can just drag their mouse down to the last cell without typing a series of numbers or dates and use the + sign to drag the variables down. When you do this, Excel automatically fills the remaining cells.

For example, let us start with the dates 01/01/2020 in cell A1 followed by 01/02/2020. There are 365 days in a year – do you really think it is a good idea to type each date in the sheet? You can use the autofill method to enter every data point in the sheet. All you need to do is drag the mouse down. You can also right click on the + sign, so you can look at the various Autofill options.

Text to Columns

There are times when you enter data into a column or copy it from another source. When you do this, Excel may copy all the data into one column. If you have to split the data, you can use the text to columns option to paste the data into different columns.

If you want to break the data into two or more columns, select the text to column option in the menu bar, and choose how you want to split the data. A dialog box opens where you can select how you want to split the data. Click Next, and then Finish, and Excel gives you the split text.

It divides the data into two columns based on your criteria. You can do this with different data sets.

Transpose

There are times when you may want to copy the data in a way that you paste the rows as columns and columns as rows. You may want to do this while you retain the format. You do not have to copy the data row by row or cell by cell. All you need to do is copy the data into the sheet using the paste special option. This option allows you to select and paste data in a specific format. Use the transpose option if you want to paste the data in this order. Consider the following example: We copy the data in Column C as rows.

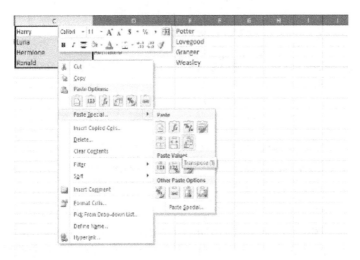

When you use the Paste Special button, you obtain the following options. The last option is Transpose, and you use this option to paste the data in a different format. Based on your selection, Excel pasted the data in the column.

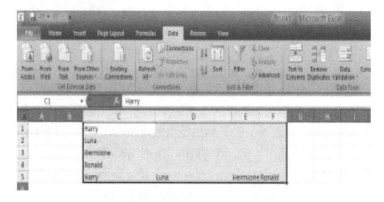

Now, look at that. That is just one of the things that Excel could do for you.

Automatically Sum Everything

We discussed the AutoSum function in the first chapter. You can use this function or option to calculate the sum of the values in the column without having to enter the formula. You can either use the AutoSum option or enter the Sum() and then hit Enter + Alt on the keyboard. This gives you the final value.

Work on Different Sheets

You know how there are different sheets in one Excel Workbook, right? Well, if they have the same layout as your original sheet, you can work on these sheets at the same time. Enter the following formula in your worksheet: =SUM('Y1:Y10'!B3) and see what happens is the workbook. When you do this, any action you perform on one sheet affects the values in the other sheet. This helps you save a lot of time since you no longer have to copy the formula across different sheets.

Display Formulas

This formula auditing method helps you to determine if a formula works correctly or not. To do this, you should display the formula and see how it works. You can use the evaluate formula option in the Formula tab to break the function down. This helps you determine whether every variable in the functions works correctly.

To do so, just click Ctrl + ` (or the acute accent key), and Excel displays the formula you used on the screen.

Conclusion

I am sure by now you understand Excel and its formulas and functions better than before.

This book explained the basics of cell referencing and how you can use these methods of referencing to use functions and formulas in Excel. You learned about the functions and formulas you can use to perform different kinds of analysis. To make it simple for you, I included some examples that hopefully helped you understand the use of the formulas and functions better.

This book shed some light on how you can use different methods of cell referencing to work with different formulas. It also talked about how you can copy and move formulas across a worksheet or workbook. As easy as it may seem, there is a good chance that you may make mistakes when you start working with Excel, so use the Formula Auditing method to determine the accuracy of a formula.

Excel is an overall important tool and through this book, I have tried my best to simplify it for you. Hopefully, you found the content helpful.

Thank you once again for choosing this book. Good luck!

Bonus

Grab your free book
https://dl.bookfunnel.com/jen2tkssx7

This book includes an overview on how each formula works along with easy to follow examples. The formulas in this book include Excel 2019 functions and are ideal for beginners through to advanced Excel users.

Get your accounts, calendars, inventory, and budgets working effortlessly with these 50 must know Excel formulas explained in *50 Most Important Formulas in Excel*. Gain valuable knowledge to put into practice and advance your Excel career.

Grab your free book
https://dl.bookfunnel.com/jen2tkssx7

References

Cheusheva, S. (2018). Using logical functions in Excel: AND, OR, XOR and NOT. Retrieved from https://www.ablebits.com/office-addins-blog/2014/12/17/excel-and-or-xor-not-functions/

Excel Ribbon - Formulas Tab. Retrieved from https://bettersolutions.com/excel/ribbon/formulas-tab.htm

Formulas and Functions in Excel. Retrieved from https://www.excel-easy.com/introduction/formulas-functions.html

Mathematical Functions - Excel 2013 - w3resource. Retrieved from https://www.w3resource.com/excel/excel-mathematical-function.php

Srivastava, H. (2018). 10 Best Uses of Microsoft Excel - Magoosh Excel Blog. Retrieved from https://magoosh.com/excel/10-best-uses-microsoft-excel/

Text functions in Excel - Type of Text functions - How to use | EduPristine. Retrieved from https://www.edupristine.com/blog/text-functions-excel

Top 15 Financial Functions in Excel | WallStreetMojo. Retrieved from https://www.wallstreetmojo.com/financial-functions-in-excel/